THE LITTLE BOOK OF

HARDCORE
Bastard
Jokes

THE LITTLE BOOK OF

HARD Bastard Jokes

Kate Kray

Pictures by Geoff Langan and Don Barrett

JOHN BLAKE

Published by John Blake Publishing Ltd, 3 Bramber Court,
2 Bramber Road, London W14 9PB, England

First published in 2003

ISBN 1 84454 002 2

British Library Cataloguing-in-Publication Data: A catalogue record for this book is
available from the British Library.

Design by ENVY

Printed and bound in Great Britain by William Clowes Ltd, Suffolk
www.clowes.co.uk

1 3 5 7 9 10 8 6 4 2

Papers used by John Blake Publishing Ltd are natural, recyclable products made from wood
grown in sustainable forests. The manufacturing processes conform to the environmental
regulations of the country of origin.

For my sister, Maggie

Acknowledgements:

A big thank you to all the men for telling me their jokes.

Thanks to Steve 'The Nostrils' Rolls.

To Geoff Langan and Don Barrett for the fantastic photos.

To Mark Hanks, my editor, for his hard work.

Introduction

All the men in Hard Bastards and Hard Bastards 2 come from a dangerous and shadowy world where life is cheap and violence is commonplace. Punchings and stabbings, knifes and shooters have long been part of their everyday existence. A lot of them still train at the gym and they always will – being fit, hard and keen is all that's between them and a trip to casualty or the city morgue. For many of them, when its six o'clock, it's time for their sharp strides. They shine their shoes, put on a crisp white shirt and adjust their dickie-bow, ready for whatever the night is going to throw at them. I've rubbed shoulders, interviewed and talked at length with literally thousands of hard bastards, gangsters, yardies, triads, terrorists, gypsies, hell's angels – you name 'em , I've interviewed 'em.

But is there a common link between them? A thread that crosses every boundary, despite colour, creed or belief? It's true that most have committed gross acts of violence, even murder. Nearly all have spent long spells in prison. Is it something in their childhood that sent them down the rocky road? Poverty? Abuse? Unhinged minds? Or are they just crazy mixed up motherfuckers? It's hard to say, and each has a different story to tell. Then it dawned on me that there was one thing that linked them all – just one.

Humour.

I don't mean that they would stab you and laugh while you bleed, (or perhaps they would!). But humour, laughter, a nudge and a grin – all of them, every single one, liked to tell a gag or two. Each man I interviewed, I asked them to tell me a joke. Instantly their faces changed. Gone was the fierce look and unblinking eyes, gone was the snarl and the spitting and cursing. Their craggy faces would lighten up. Broad gold-toothed smiles beamed at me –' 'ere, do you know that one about … knock knock … An Englishman, an Irishman and a Scotsman … '

After they delivered the punchline, all would crease up, howling with laughter. They would look around the room, expecting everyone to find the joke as funny as they did. Some would titter a nervous titter, some would laugh out of fear of losing their bollocks. All in all, everyone laughed. Here is a collection of those jokes.

Kate Kray.

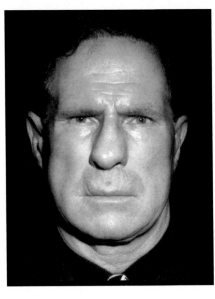

Photography © Don Barret

NAME: **Roy Shaw**

DATE OF BIRTH: **You're as old as the woman you feel!**

STAR SIGN: **Pisces**

OCCUPATION: **Whatever he wants!**

DID YOU HEAR about the two convicts in America who were about to be executed? The warden says to the first one, 'Do you have a last request?' The convict says, 'Yes, I'd like to hear the song "Achy Breaky Heart" one last time.' The Warden says, 'OK, I think we can arrange that.' Then he says to the second convict, 'How about you?' The second convict says, 'Yeah, kill me first.'

NAME: Vic Dark

DATE OF BIRTH: 12 April 1957

STAR SIGN: Aries

OCCUPATION: Ex-armed robber

THERE'S A NEW PRODUCT on the market – Viagra eye drops.
They don't do anything, just make you look hard.

NAME: Joey Pyle

DATE OF BIRTH: 2 November 1937

STAR SIGN: Scorpio

OCCUPATION: Businessman

A MAFIA GODFATHER, accompanied by his attorney, walks into a room to meet with his former accountant. The Godfather asks the accountant, 'Where is the 3 million bucks you embezzled from me?' The accountant does not answer. The Godfather asks again, 'Where is the 3 million bucks you embezzled from me?' The attorney interrupts, 'Sir, the man is a deaf mute and cannot understand you, but I can interpret for you.' The Godfather says, 'Well ask him where my damn money is!' The attorney, using sign language, asks the accountant where the 3 million dollars is. The accountant signs back, 'I don't know what you are talking about.' The attorney interprets to the Godfather, 'He doesn't know what you are talking about.' The Godfather pulls out a .9 mm pistol, puts it to the temple of the accountant, cocks the trigger and says, 'Ask him again where my damn money is!' The attorney signs to the accountant, 'He wants to know where it is!' The accountant signs back, 'OK! OK! OK! The money is hidden in a brown suitcase behind the shed in my backyard!' The Godfather says, 'Well ...what did he say? 'The attorney interprets to the Godfather, 'He says ... go to hell ... that you don't have the guts to pull the trigger.'

7

NAME: **Freddie Foreman**

DATE OF BIRTH: **5 March 1932**

STAR SIGN: **Pisces**

OCCUPATION: **Managing Director of British Crime**

After checking the licence of the driver he'd stopped,
the police officer comments. 'It says here you're supposed to be
wearing glasses.' 'But Officer,' said the driver, 'I've got contacts.'
'I don't care who you know,' snaps the officer. 'You're breaking
the law.'

NAME: Kevin Houston – 'naughty but nice'

DATE OF BIRTH: 8 May 1951

STAR SIGN: Taurus

OCCUPATION: Boxing Promoter; Tattoo Artist; Entrepreneur

THERE'S THIS PRIEST, and he's having a wank at the back of the Vatican, and he hears a click – and there's a tourist who is taking a picture of him. So he says, 'Oh, you have a camera,' and the tourist says, 'Yes, I take picture of you.' The priest says, 'How much do you want for camera?' He says, 'A thousand dollars.' The priest says, 'OK, I give you a thousand dollars for camera.' So he gives him the thousand dollars and gets the fucking camera from him and walks round the corner and sees the Monsignor. The Monsignor says, 'How much you pay for the camera?' The priest says, 'I pay a thousand dollars for camera.' The Monsignor says, 'He must have seen you coming!'

NAME: Bill – 'It's not over till it's over'

DATE OF BIRTH: 15 December 1961

STAR SIGN: Sagittarius

OCCUPATION: Personal security for the stars

WHAT DO YOU call an Indian Lesbian?
Mingeater.

Did you hear about the flasher who was thinking of retiring?
He decided to stick it out for one more year.

What did the banana say to the vibrator?
What are you shaking for? She's going to eat me!

NAME: **Charlie Bronson**

DATE OF BIRTH: **6 December 1951**

STAR SIGN: **Sagittarius**

OCCUPATION: **Hostage-taker, serving life imprisonment**

HERE'S ONE FOR you. Fact.

Fred West, 'the nonce', was two cells away from me in
Winson Green. I used to look through the spy hole in his door. He
looked like that Benny out of Crossroads – simple, the village
idiot – two cans short of a six-pack type. One day I shouted
through his door, 'Oi, Fred. They've just found two skeletons up
your chimney!' He looked at me with those big, sad puppy eyes.
Then I shouted, 'Don't worry about it, it's probably
two old flames!' I used to love winding him up!

What do you call an escaped lunatic with a chainsaw?
Sir.

NAME: Johnny Adair

DATE OF BIRTH: 27 October 1963

STAR SIGN:: Scorpio

OCCUPATION: Terrorist

There were two eggs in a saucepan and they were boiling away. One says to the other, 'Cor, it's hot in here,' and the other says, 'That's nothing, when we get out of here we're going to get our heads smashed in!'

NAME: John Daniels – 'A Man Mountain, an immovable object'

DATE OF BIRTH: I never reveal my age

STAR SIGN: Libra

OCCUPATION: Enforcer

One day, this lorry driver was motoring along a country road and he saw a priest walking along the grass verge, so he stopped to see if he wanted a lift. 'Where are you going, Father?' he asked him. 'To the church five miles down the road,' the priest replied. 'OK father, hop in. So the priest climbed into the passenger seat and they drove on. Suddenly the lorry driver saw a lawyer walking along the pavement and as usual he swerved to get him. But then he remembered he had a priest with him and he swerved back, narrowly missing the lawyer. But he heard a loud noise – 'Thud!' The Lorry driver was a bit puzzled and he glanced in his rear mirror, but he couldn't see anything. 'Sorry about that, father,' he said to the priest, 'I nearly hit that lawyer.' 'That's OK, son,' said the priest. 'I got him with the door.'

NAME: **Carlton Leach**

DATE OF BIRTH: **1 March 1959**

STAR SIGN: **Pisces**

OCCUPATION: **Enforcer**

There's three ducks and one of them goes into a pub and up to the bar. The geezer behind the bar says, 'What's your name, Mate?' and the duck says 'My name is Dave.' So the bartender says, 'What have you been up to today, Dave?' The duck says, 'I've had a lovely day, I've been in and out of puddles and having a laugh. I'll have a pint of lager please.' Another duck walks in, he goes, 'My name's Steve.' So the bartender says, 'How have you been, Steve? What you been up to?' And Steve says, 'I've had a lovely day, I've been in and out of puddles and all that.' The bartender says, 'Do you want a drink?' Steve says, 'Yeah, I'll have a drink, I'll have a lager.' Then the next duck walks in and the barman says to him, 'All right, mate. What's your name?' And the duck says, 'My name's Puddles. Fuck off!'

Photography © Geoff Langan

NAME: John Pierre Rollinson – 'Gaffer'

DATE OF BIRTH: 5 April 1951

STAR SIGN: Aries

OCCUPATION: Professional lazy bastard!

Did you know that if you ain't circumcised you can't
join the police force because you ain't a complete prick!

A man gets arrested. 'Anything you say will be taken
down as evidence,' says the copper.
'Stop hitting me with that truncheon!' says the man.

My wife said to me, 'You knock about with your best
mate so much - how would you like it if I went to bed
with him?'
'I would call you a lesbian,' I said.

I got home early and jumped into bed with my wife.
'Shit,' she shouted, 'My husband's home!'
Like a dick I jumped out the window.

NAME: **Stellakis Stylianou – Stilks**

DATE OF BIRTH: **21 July 1958**

STAR SIGN: **I'm a Cancerian, born on the cusp, and I like to think I'm more of a Leo**

OCCUPATION: **Professional doorman**

What do you do if your girlfriend starts smoking?
Slow down and use a lubricant

What you call a gay dinosaur?
A Megasorearse

I went to a dyslexic rave. I got out of my head on an F.

What did the elephant say to the naked man?
How can you breathe through that?

What do you call a dog with no legs?
Anything – he ain't coming anyway!

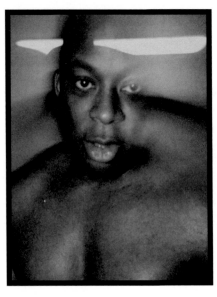

Photography © Geoff Langan

NAME: Ian Wadley

DATE OF BIRTH: 24 March 1966

STAR SIGN: Aries

OCCUPATION: Fixer

Two old geezers are talking about Viagra. One has never heard of it and asks the other what it's for. 'It's the greatest invention ever,' he said. 'It makes you feel like a man of 30.'

'Can you get it over the counter?'

'Probably – if you took two.'

NAME: Tony Lambrianou

DATE OF BIRTH: 15 April 1947

STAR SIGN: Aries

OCCUPATION: Ex-gangster

One morning a blind bunny rabbit was hopping down the bunny trail when he tripped over a large snake. 'Oh please excuse me,' said the little bunny. 'I didn't mean to trip over you, but I'm blind and can't see where I'm going.' 'That's perfectly all right,' says the snake. 'It was my fault. I didn't mean to trip you, but I'm blind too and I didn't see you coming. By the way, what kind of animal are you?' 'Well, I really don't know,' replied the bunny. 'I've never seen myself. Maybe you could examine me and find out.' So the snake felt the rabbit all over and he said, 'Well, you're soft and cuddly, and you have long silky ears and a little fluffy tail, you must be a bunny rabbit.' Then the rabbit said, 'I can't thank you enough. By the way, what kind of animal are you?' The snake replied that he didn't know, and the bunny agreed to examine him. When he was finished the snake said, 'What kind of animal am I?' And the Bunny, who had felt him all over, replied, 'You're hard, you're cold, you're slimy and you haven't got any balls – you must be a lawyer!'

NAME: **Kiane Sabert**

DATE OF BIRTH: **9 March 1973**

STAR SIGN: **Pisces**

OCCUPATION: **PBG (Personal Bodyguard)**

A man went to the police station demanding to speak with the burglar who had broken into his house the previous night. 'You'll get your chance in court,' said the desk sergeant. 'No, you don't understand,' said the man. 'I want to know how he got into the house in the middle of the night without waking my wife. I've been trying to do that for years.'

31

NAME: **Gary Hunter**

DATE OF BIRTH: **30 September 1963**

STAR SIGN: **Libra**

OCCUPATION: **Bodyguard**

What is the similarity between a lawyer and a sperm?
Only one in a million turns out to be human.

NAME: Sid the knife – just call me Sid – that will do

DATE OF BIRTH: 21 March 1964

STAR SIGN: Aries

OCCUPATION: Transport driver, ex-doorman

An man goes to a fancy dress party with a blond draped over his shoulder. 'I've come as a tortoise,' he says, and points to the girl on his back, 'and this is Michelle.'

Photography © Geoff Langan

NAME: **Baz Allen**

DATE OF BIRTH: **28 July 1967**

STAR SIGN: **Leo – a real Leo**

OCCUPATION: **Minder/Enforcer for the firm. I also work for myself and for a famous Indian family who do hundreds of millions of pounds' worth of business. Say no more**

A Mexican, an Irishman, an African, a kilted Scotsman, a priest, two lesbians, a rabbi and a nun walk into a bar. The landlord looks up and says, 'What the hell is this, some kind of joke?'

NAME: **Kevin Chan**

DATE OF BIRTH: **11 June 1967**

STAR SIGN: **Gemini**

OCCUPATION: **Kung-Fu Master and instructor**

What do you say to a man with two black eyes?
Nothing. He's already been told twice.

NAME: Daniel Reece

DATE OF BIRTH: 24 June 1956

STAR SIGN: Cancer

OCCUPATION: Robber

Police in Birmingham had good luck with a robbery suspect who just couldn't control himself during a line-up. When detectives asked each man in the line-up to repeat the words, 'Give me all your money or I'll shoot,' the bloke shouted, 'that's not what I said!'

Photography © Geoff Langan

NAME: **Chris Murphy**

DATE OF BIRTH: **9 October 1956**

STAR SIGN: **Libra**

OCCUPATION: **He ain't letting on!**

'My uncle in Essex tried to make a new kind of car. He took the engine from a Ford, the transmission from an Oldsmobile, the tyres from a Cadillac, and the exhaust system from a Plymouth.'
'Really? What did he get?'
'Fifteen years.'

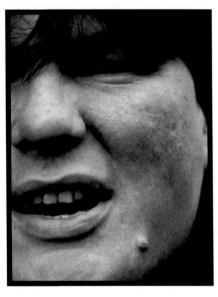

NAME: Dave Davis

DATE OF BIRTH: 14 April 1969

STAR SIGN: Aries

OCCUPATION: Security adviser

A young man was taking a verbal test to join the local police force. The question asked, 'If you were driving a police car alone on a lonely road at night and were being chased by a gang of criminals driving sixty miles an hour, what would you do?'

The young man answered without a second's thought: 'Seventy!'

NAME: Jamie O'Keefe

DATE OF BIRTH: 29 April 1961

STAR SIGN: Taurus

OCCUPATION: Author of self-protection books; social care worker for young people with challenging behaviour.

A geezer and his wife are cooing over their new born baby.

'Look at his todger,' says the man. 'It's massive!'

'Yes dear,' says the woman. 'But at least he's got your eyes.'

NAME: **Trevor Roberts – The Iron Man of Bolton**

DATE OF BIRTH: **19 January 1950**

STAR SIGN: **Capricorn**

OCCUPATION: **Security Director**

One bloke sent to prison wasn't worried at all about serving his full term. When asked why, he said his wife had never let him finish a sentence the whole time they'd been married.

NAME: **Brian Thorogood**

DATE OF BIRTH: **22 December 1938**

STAR SIGN: **Capricorn**

OCCUPATION: **Armed Robber**

Two young kids were talking to each other. They were both little liars and one says, 'I jumped off that 100-foot cliff yesterday,' and the other says, 'I know you did, I saw you.'

An Irishman went into a bar. 'Aaaaargh', he went.
It was an iron bar.

NAME : Marco

DATE OF BIRTH : 7 September 1952

STAR SIGN : Virgo

OCCUPATION : Licensee and Hell's Angel

A bloke walks into a pub with a yellow, long-nosed, short-legged dog under his arm. 'That's one ugly dog,' says another patron, petting his Doberman. 'Well he might be ugly, but he's a mean little bastard.' 'Is that so?' says the other patron, 'I'll bet you £50 my dog will kick his arse in less than two minutes.' The bloke agrees, so they put their dogs face to face and each gives the command to attack. In the twinkling of an eye, the little yellow dog has bitten the Doberman clean in half. 'Fuck' shouts the Doberman's devastated owner. 'He killed Fang! What kind of fucking dog is this?' 'Well,' says the bloke, 'before I cut off his tail and painted him yellow he was a crocodile.'

NAME:: **Kalvinder Dhesi – Kal**

DATE OF BIRTH: **24 July 1965**

STAR SIGN: **Leo**

OCCUPATION: **Door supervisor in Rochester**

It was the stockbroker's first day in prison and on meeting his psychotic-looking cellmate he became even more nervous than ever. 'Don't worry mate,' said the prisoner when he noticed how scared the stockbroker looked. 'I'm in for a white collar crime, too' 'Oh, really?' said the stockbroker with a sigh of relief. 'Yeah,' said the prisoner. 'I murdered a priest.'

NAME: Lou Yates

DATE OF BIRTH: 3 June 1951

STAR SIGN: Leo

OCCUPATION: Doorman and bare-knuckle fighter

A man thinks he's a dog, so off he trots to see a psychiatrist. 'It's a nightmare,' he says, 'I walk around on all fours, I bark all night and I can't walk past lamp-posts no more.' 'OK,' says the shrink. 'Get on the couch.' The man replies: 'I'm not allowed on the couch.'

**NAME : Dominic – Why do you want to know?
Can I call my solicitor?**

DATE OF BIRTH : **28 July 1970**

STAR SIGN : **Leo**

OCCUPATION : **I'm a professional fighter and
that's it – honest!**

How do you turn a fox into an elephant?
Marry it.

NAME: **Manchester Tony.**

DATE OF BIRTH: **4 March 1962**

STAR SIGN: **Pisces.**

OCCUPATION: **Gym owner and doorman.**

A wife asks her husband why he never calls out her name while they're at it. The husband shrugs, takes her hand and says, 'Because I don't want to wake you.'

Photography © Don Barret

NAME: Cornish Mick

DATE OF BIRTH: 10 February 1935

STAR SIGN: Aquarius

OCCUPATION: Gangster

A new man is brought into Prison Cell 102. Already there is a long-time resident who looks 100 years old. The new man looks at the old-timer inquiringly. The old-timer says, 'Look at me. I'm old and worn out. You'd never believe that I used to live the life of Riley. I wintered on the Riviera, had a boat, four fine cars, the most beautiful women, and I ate in all the best restaurants of France.' The new man asked, 'What happened?' 'One day Riley reported his credit cards missing.'

NAME: Noel Ennis – 'The ex-King of Mean'

DATE OF BIRTH: 25 December 1958

STAR SIGN: Capricorn

OCCUPATION: General Manager

A man walks into a pub with a frog on his head, and the barman says, 'Where did you get that from?' And the frog says, 'It started off as a wart on my arse!'

Photography © Geoff Langan

NAME: Stevie Knock – 'Knock-out knock'

DATE OF BIRTH: 18 April 1967

STAR SIGN: Aquarius

OCCUPATION: Former Doorman

What's pink and hard?

A pig with a flick knife

This old geezer's lying on his death bed and his old woman comes to visit him. His name is Manny and he says to her, 'Gloria, I'm on my death bed and after all these years you've stuck with me.' She says, 'I have.' And he says, 'Gloria, I was having it off with that young bird in the village and then she left me and you stuck with me.' She says, 'I did.' And he says, 'I went to war and lost an arm and a leg and you still stuck with me' She says, 'I did.' 'Now I'm on my deathbed, you're still by my side. Why don't you just fuck off, you're a fucking jinx!'

Photography © Don Barret

NAME:Frasier Tranter

DATE OF BIRTH:17 November 1965

STAR SIGN:Scorpio

OCCUPATION:Proprietor of a security company and World Strongman contender

A man phoned the hospital in a state of excitement.
'My wife is pregnant. Her contractions are only two minutes
apart. 'The doctor said: 'Is this her first child?'
'No, you twat. This is her husband.'

Photography © Don Barret

NAME:: **Cass Pennant**

DATE OF BIRTH: **3 March 1958**

STAR SIGN: **Pisces**

OCCUPATION: **Writer, Businessman and ex-leader of the ICF**

Two rats in a sewer been eating shit all day. One says, 'I'm sick of eating shit every single day!' 'Cheer up,' says his mate, 'We're on the piss tonight!'

A boy asked his Mum, 'Is it wrong to have a willy?'
'No. Why?' she replies.
'Well, Dad's sweating like fuck trying to pull his off!'

NAME : **The Bower Brothers – Martin, Tony and Paul Bower**

DATE OF BIRTH : **Tony: 15 August 1958, Martin: 18 February 1965 Paul: 8 March 1967**

STAR SIGN : **Tony: Leo, Martin: Aquarius, Paul: Pisces**

OCCUPATION : **Entrepreneurs**

Freddie Mercury dies and the Angel Gabriel goes to Freddie and says, 'Freddie I loved your music so much I want you to go back downstairs. Obviously you can't go back as Freddie Mercury or else you'll be missed in heaven, so you've got to pick someone else and I'll put you down as him.' So Freddie has a think and he says, 'Angel Gabriel, I would like to be the Arsenal goalkeeper.' The Angel Gabriel turns round and says, 'What a strange choice, you could have been anyone – Brad Pitt maybe or any of the top models, why the fuck do you want to be David Seaman?' And Freddie says, 'It's quite simple. I'll have eleven arseholes in front of me and thousands of dicks behind me!'

Photography © Don Barret

NAME: **Ronnie Field**

DATE OF BIRTH: **9 August 1946**

STAR SIGN: **Leo**

OCCUPATION: **Armed Robber**

Two fellas are fishing in a boat under a bridge. One looks up and sees a funeral procession starting across the bridge. He stands up, takes off his cap, and bows his head. The procession crosses the bridge and the man puts on his cap, picks up his rod and reel, and continues fishing. The other guy says, 'That was touching. I didn't know you had it in you.' The first guy responds, 'Well, I guess it was the thing to do - after all, I was married to her for 40 years.'

NAME: **Felix Ntumazah**

DATE OF BIRTH: **29 August 1962**

STAR SIGN: **Virgo**

OCCUPATION: **British Karate Champion**

A young man, kind of a biker, had started to work on a farm. The boss sent him to the back forty to do some fencing work, but come evening he's half an hour late. The boss gets on the CB radio to check if he's all right. 'I've got a problem, Boss. I'm stuck here. I've hit a pig!' said the young man. 'Ah well, these things happen sometimes,' the boss says. 'Just drag the carcass off the road so nobody else hits it in the dark.' 'But he's not dead, boss. He's gotten tangled up on the bull bar, and I've tried to untangle him, but he's kicking and squealing, and he's real big boss. I'm afraid he's gonna hurt me!' 'Never mind,' says the boss. 'There's a .303 under the tarp in the back. Get that out and shoot him. Then drag the carcass off the road and come on home.' 'Okay, boss,' said the young man. Another half an hour goes by, but there's still not a peep from the kid. The boss gets back on the CB. 'What's the problem, son?' 'Well, I did what you said boss, but I'm still stuck,' replied the young man. 'What's up? Did you drag the pig off the road like I said?' asked the boss. The young man replied, 'Yeah boss, but his motorcycle is still jammed under the truck.'

NAME: **Bobby Wren**

DATE OF BIRTH: **26 October 1959**

STAR SIGN: **Scorpio**

OCCUPATION: **SAS**

A huge fleet of the English army came to a hill, on the bottom of the hill, there was a forest of trees. Just before the king was about to go down into it he heard a voice from the forest. It yelled, ' ONE IRISH MAN WILL DEFEAT THE WHOLE ENGLISH ARMY!! 'The king was outraged and he sent two of his best knights down. After much clashing of swords there was blood-curdling screams and all was silent. Again the king heard 'ONE IRISH MAN WILL DEFEAT THE WHOLE ENGLISH ARMY!!' He was now so furious that he sent twenty of his knights down. There were screams of agony and pain ... then all was quiet. Again they heard 'ONE IRISH MAN WILL DEFEAT THE WHOLE ENGLISH ARMY!!' The king was now seeing red and in his fury he sent the remaining of his fleet down to the forest. There were screams and clashing of swords and then all was quiet. The king was dumbfounded!! But one of his comrades came limping up the hill, this man was tattered and bruised, his left hand had been chopped off and he was bleeding profusely. In a hoarse voice he knelt before the king and said, 'My lord they tricked us ... there were two of them.'

79

NAME: **Harry H**

DATE OF BIRTH: **29 November 1956**

STAR SIGN: **Sagittarius**

OCCUPATION: **Gentleman villain**

One day a guy died and found himself in hell. As he was wallowing in despair, he had his first meeting with a demon. The demon asked, 'Why so glum?' The guy responded, 'What do you think? I'm in hell!' 'Hell's not so bad,' the demon said. 'We actually have a lot of fun down here. You a drinking man?' 'Sure,' the man said, 'I love to drink.' 'Well you're gonna love Mondays then. On Mondays all we do is drink. Whiskey, tequila, Guinness, wine coolers, diet Tab and Fresca. We drink till we throw up and then we drink some more!' The guy is astounded. 'Damn, that sounds great.' 'You a smoker?' the demon asked. 'You better believe it!' 'You're gonna love Tuesdays. We get the finest cigars from all over the world and smoke our lungs out. If you get cancer, no biggie. You're already dead, remember?' The demon continued. 'I bet you like to gamble.' 'Why yes, as a matter of fact I do.' 'Wednesdays you can gamble all you want. Craps, blackjack, roulette, poker, slots, whatever. If you go bankrupt, well, you're dead anyhow'. You into drugs?' The guy said, 'Are you kidding? I love drugs! You don't mean...?' 'That's right! Thursday is drug day. Help yourself to a great big bowl of crack, or smack. Smoke a doobie the size of a submarine. You can do all the drugs you want, you're dead, who cares!' 'Wow,' the guy said, starting to feel better about his situation, 'I never realised Hell was such a cool place!' The demon said, 'You gay?' 'No,' came the reply. 'Ooooh, you're gonna hate Fridays!'

NAME: **John McGinnis**

DATE OF BIRTH: **19 September 1954**

STAR SIGN: **Virgo**

OCCUPATION: **Doorman**

There was this guy in a bar one night and he drank and drank until the bar closed. By the time the bar tender chucked him out he was so pissed he was paraletic. He stumbled out onto the foot path and walking a few metres away from him was a nun. He staggered over to the nun and immediately started throwing wild punches at her, he connected with several big hits and the nun hit the footpath out cold, the drunk then proceeded to kick the nun several times. Exhausted after his drunken efforts, the man bent down and put his face up to the nun's and said, 'Not so tough after all are you batman.'

Photography © Don Barret

NAME: **Errol Francis**

DATE OF BIRTH: **21 July 1956**

STAR SIGN:: **Leo, on the cusp of cancer**

OCCUPATION: **Celebrity Minder**

A little paper bag was feeling unwell, so he took himself off to the doctors. 'Doctor, I don't feel too good,' said the little paper bag. 'Hmm, you look OK to me,' said the Doctor, 'but I'll do a blood test and see what that shows, come back and see me in a couple of days'. The little paper bag felt no better when he got back for the results. 'What's wrong with me?' asked the little paper bag. 'I'm afraid you are HIV positive!' said the doctor. 'No, I can't be – I'm just a little paper bag!' said the little paper bag. 'Have you been having unprotected sex?' asked the doctor. 'NO, I can't do things like that – I'm just a little paper bag!' 'Well have you been sharing needles with other intravenous drug users?' asked the doctor. 'NO, I can't do things like that – I'm just a little paper bag!' 'Perhaps you've been abroad recently and required a jab or a blood transfusion?' queried the doctor. 'NO, I don't have a passport – I'm just a little paper bag!' 'Well', said the doctor, 'are you in a homosexual relationship?' 'NO! I told you I can't do things like that – I'm just a little paper bag!' 'Then there can be only one explanation,' said the doctor 'Your mother must have been a carrier.'

NAME: Glenn Ross

DATE OF BIRTH: 27 May 1971

STAR SIGN: Gemini

OCCUPATION: Doorman. I used to be a chef, specialising in wedding cakes, but I gave it up to become a full-time strongman.

A man was in court for a double murder, and the judge said, 'You are charged with beating your wife to death with a hammer.' A voice at the back of the courtroom yelled out, 'You bastard!' The judge continued, 'You are also charged with beating your mother-in-law to death with a hammer.' Again, the voice at the back of the courtroom yelled out, 'You damned bastard!' The judge stopped, looked at the man in the back of the courtroom, and said, 'Sir, I can understand your anger and frustration at this crime, but I will not have any more of these outbursts from you, or I shall charge you with contempt! Now is that a problem?' The man at the back of the court stood up and responded, 'For fifteen years, I have lived next door to that bastard, and every time I asked to borrow a hammer, he said he never had one!'

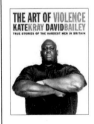